Unique & Unusual *Pens*

from the Wood Lathe

DICK SING

Text written with and photography by Alison Levie

Schiffer Publishing Ltd

4880 Lower Valley Road, Atglen, PA 19310 USA

Dedication

To Jacob Richard Powers
My grandson, who has become Papa's second
shadow and the second edition of Grandma's most
expensive toys.

Copyright © 1997 by Dick Sing
Library of Congress Catalog Card Number: 97-67030

Book Designed by Laurie A. Smucker

Printed in China
ISBN: 0-7643-0359-7

Published by Schiffer Publishing Ltd.
4880 Lower Valley Road
Atglen, PA 19310
Phone: (610) 593-1777; Fax: (610) 593-2002
E-mail:Schifferbk@aol.com
Please write for a free catalog.
This book may be purchased from the publisher.
Please include $3.95 for shipping.
Try your bookstore first.

We are interested in hearing from authors
with book ideas on related subjects.

Contents

Acknowledgments

Thank you to the following companies who helped make this book possible: The Berea Hardwood Co., Brook Park, Ohio; Bonhams Woodworking supply, Inc., Garland, Texas; Craft Supplies U.S.A., Provo, Utah ; Hut Products for Wood, Sturgeon, Missouri; One Good Turn, Murray, Utah; Packard Woodworks, Tyron, NC; Woodcuts Ltd., Racine, Wisconsin; Woodcraft Supply Corp., Parkersburg, WV.

Gallery set-up by Cindy Sing.

Introduction

Changes occur quickly in the turning world. Pen kits, materials, tools, lathes, ideas, processes, and glues change. People get bored. They want something new to do. Competition against other turners, ego trips, something new to take to the club, experience—all these create a demand for new pens.

Since Pens from the Wood Lathe came out, the interest in pens has continued to climb, and I have continued to look for new ways to develop unique and unusual pens. This book provides some new pens, and lots of new ways to make old pens. Some of these pens will challenge the skills of the woodturner. Sharp tools, a light touch, and practice should make any of the pens in this book possible.

I encourage you to try your own shapes and contours.

Listen to people when they look at your pens, watch their reactions, and ask for input. You may come up with some great ideas trying to meet someone's individual desire. Visualize the pen before you assemble it. Look at the end grain; lay pieces next to a finished pen; think about what you want; then think again. At the same time, be looking for new ideas. Keep an open mind, and recognize that anything can stimulate a creative spark. Most important, keep paper handy. No matter how small or trivial the idea, write it down. If you don't, your idea may well be gone when you need to use it.

If while trying some of these pens, you make mistakes, don't be discouraged. Use your mistakes to learn and improve your product.

Woods

The wood you choose for anything as small as a pen needs to be carefully selected, but the size and shape of the pen provides some wonderful opportunities for creative and striking effects to make something unusual.

Sapwood and Heartwood

The sapwood, found between the bark and the heartwood at the center of the tree, is always lighter than the heartwood, and normally is a different tone than any of the heartwoods. Some sapwood can be very striking. Because it is often soft, the sapwood is not always usable and is susceptible to powder beetles. However, the beetle holes can be filled for contrast, and soft wood can be stabilized.

Dramatic color combinations are possible with pens made from blanks containing both heartwood and sapwood. With linear grain heartwood and sapwood, the grain normally runs parallel, and can be cut straight to the axis of the pen, or the blank can be cut using the end grain.

End Grain Cuts

A blank cut using the end grain—at a 90º angle to the grain requires sound wood with good contrast and pattern. When we use the end grain, the fibers are only as long as the wood on the pen barrel is thick. The lack of strength in the grain results in easy mishaps. Gluing can also be more difficult on end grain. However, the end grain usually takes an easy, high luster finish and the results can be well worth the extra effort. Sapwood and heartwood combinations cut this way can provide some of the most striking contrasts and patterns available in natural materials. I try to use two blanks next to each other to keep the colors and patterns uniform in the pen. This is not a hard rule as I have seen the top and bottom halves of different grain patterns and even altogether different woods combined with striking results.

> **TIP**: To increase the strength with end grain wood on the straight rollerball pen, apply a coat of thin hot stuff (cyanacrylate) to the end grain after trimming. Then lightly retrim. This will saturate and fill the pores.

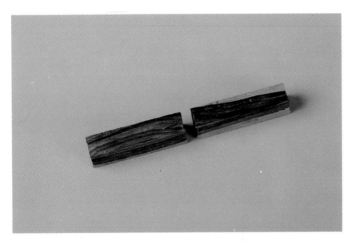

A blank cut from Cocobolo heartwood, sapwood combination with parallel grain.

Granadillo with a blister grain pattern showing heartwood and sapwood combination.

These Cocobolo blanks were cut 90º to the normal parallel grain direction. The contrasting grains now run around the pen instead of down the length of the pen. The placement of the sapwood can be either at the ends or in the middle of the pen, creating fascinating contrasts and variety.

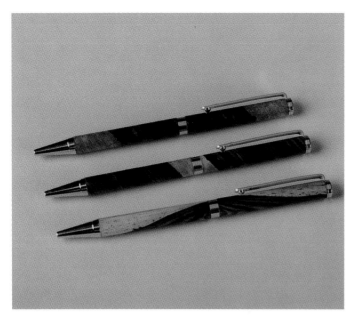

The pens from Cocobolo heartwood and sapwood. The top pen shows the end grain at a 90° angle to the axis of the pen, with the sapwood on the ends of the pen and the heartwood in the middle. The middle pen has the end grain with the sapwood in the middle and the heartwood on the ends. The bottom pen has the grain running parallel to the axis of the pen.

End grain in Spalted Cherry.

Angled Grain Cuts

Angled grain cuts provide another opportunity for striking grain patterns, plus they allow smaller pieces to be used because grain patterns do not show a distinctive mismatch. However, working with angled grain blanks provides special challenges. They are more difficult to drill as the drill tends to skate in the direction of least resistance, and gluing involves the same problems as does end grain gluing. Turning also requires special care, as one side of the blank is straight grain and the other half is end grain.

Bocote wood with blanks marked to establish angled grain alignment.

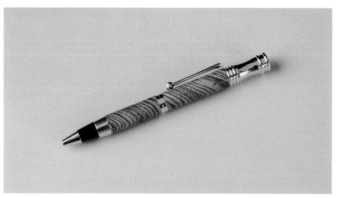

The pen turned from the angled Bocote blanks.

Burl

Burl is a growth on the tree, which, because it is not a part of the normal growth of the tree, has its own grain direction. Its grain has no rhyme or reason, so again it can be a little more difficult to work with, but provides the opportunity for something different.

This slab, cut from Amboyna burl shows how the grain pattern was established on the burl. The black lines mark the cuts used to create a blank like the one on the right.

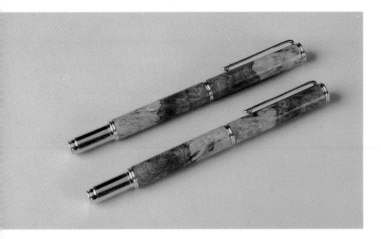

Pens cut from the Amboyna burl. One of the pens has the heartwood in the center, the other has the heartwood on the ends.

Other Special Qualities in Wood

Wood provides many opportunities to find special qualities that create beautiful effects. Look for wood with chatoyant characteristics—the reflective quality within the wood that has a changeable luster or color.

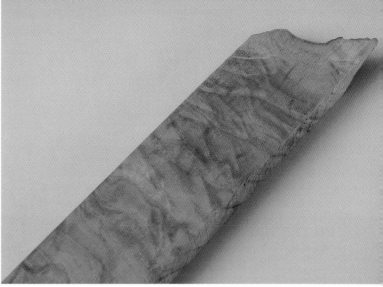

Slab taken from a crotch area of a Walnut tree. Excellent example of chatoyancy.

Classic rollerball pen using the walnut.

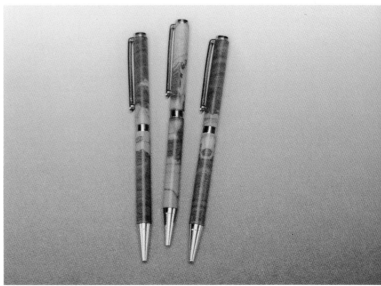

These three pens were all cut from the same board of Spalted Cherry wood. Note the marked difference in appearance.

Materials Other than Wood

Acrylic Acetate, Celluloid Acetate, Decora, Crushed Velvet

These materials are constantly changing as more colors, patterns, and compositions become available. They glue easily, cut easily, and produce their own finish through buffing. Don't use coarse abrasives in the initial sanding because they will scratch.

Corian®

Again, new colors and patterns are constantly being developed. Products similar to Corian, but made by different manufacturers, vary in consistency and cutting properties.

Dymondwood

Dymondwood is composed of layers of birch, dyed with aniline dyes and put together with epoxies, heat, and high pressure. The result is a durable, attractive product in a variety of patterns, from showy to natural, that contains its own finish. Each batch can change color and consistency.

Pickguard and Knife Spacer Veneer

This is laminated plastic and combinations of plastic used in the musical instrument industry and for custom knife making. These materials can be used as accent pieces in the pens.

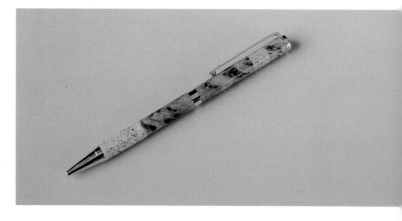

Corian and Hornbean burl. Different contrasts.

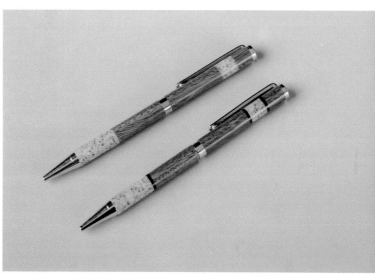

Top pen: Corian and Vera Wood. Bottom pen: Corian, Vera Wood, with the addition of black pickguard material for accent.

Sample patterns of combined Corian and Ironwood to show some of the different effects of contrast between spacing of materials.

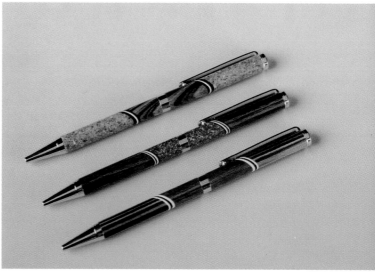

Combinations of Dymondwood and Corian, cut on an angle with inserts of pickguard material for accent.

Dymondwood with straight grain and Corian.

Stabilized or Impregnated Wood

Borderline or unstable wood, or even perfect wood, can be treated by stabilization. The wood is impregnated with epoxies and resins under high pressure and cured with heat. Color can be introduced during the process as well. Not all woods accept the process equally, and color penetration can vary throughout the blank based on hardness and grain pattern.

Antler

Antler is a living material, like wood. No two pieces are alike. The habitat of an animal can have an effect on color and density, as can the species or breed. Elk has more marrow and therefore is often more colorful from the dried blood in the marrow. The deer antler, which is normally a smaller diameter, will produce a much denser, more ivory-like surface, especially in smaller diameters. I like to use polyurethane glue to glue the brass tubes into the antler as the glue is opaque and expands to fill the pores in the antler, which helps hide the brass tube.

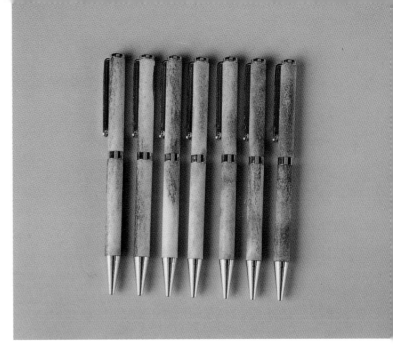

Straight pens made from various deer antlers show contrasts in colors.

Tagua Nut

Tagua nuts, also known as vegetable ivory, are a legal substitute for ivory with similar appearance. They provide a unique material for contrast and accent.

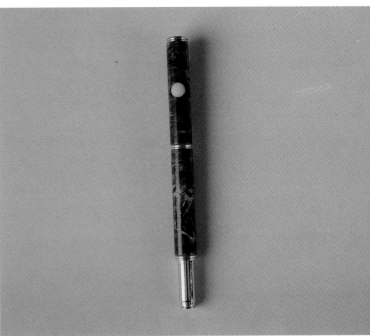

Roller ball pen from maple burl which has been stabilized and dyed blue with tagua dot.

Cast Polyester

Cast polyester is a manufactured material made to duplicate ivory, bone, animal horn, tortoise shell, onyx, and black marble. It cuts, glues, and works easily, and has a fine finish. It is also available in sizes large enough to make a complete pen.

Roller ball style pens made from the antler of an elk.

Filling Voids

Cyanoacrylate can be used for minor defects such as cracks, pits, and voids. For larger voids, fill the voids with a little matching dust to provide a more natural look, or use epoxy and pigments to create a color contrast. If you do use epoxy to fill voids, use the long term epoxy, as air bubbles have time to work themselves out before the epoxy becomes stiff, trapping the bubbles which create voids in the glue itself.

A third alternative for large voids, whether natural or purposely made for inlays, is to use ground stone, malachite, coral, etc. This can either be mixed in with epoxy or the material can be put into the void and flooded with cyanoacrylate. If you use cyanoacrylate do not hit with the accelerator immediately or a residue may remain. Since these stone or mineral fill materials generally do not cut or sand well, before using any of them, reduce the diameter of the blank close to its finished dimension and try to keep the level of the materials below the surface of the wood. Unlike chips or flakes, powdered fill materials are less likely to lift out while cutting.

The bottles are colored pigments and the bag is malachite powder.

Tools

Gouges

A 3/8" spindle gouge is a very important tool. It is one of the better tools to use for roughing, and, by pulling the ears (the corners of the gouge) back, the gouge can be used for a shear cut. A 1/4" spindle gouge is sometimes very useful for detailing or situations where nothing seems to work.

Don't force gouges. Use a light touch and allow the tool to do the cutting. Learn to master the gouge for it has a multitude of ways to be used—both traditional and inventive.

Skews

Skews are frustrating, cantankerous SOB's until they are mastered, but a skew is an essential and rewarding tool needed by a pen turner. With proper handling they cut a flat plain or curve like no other tool. The tip of a skew can also be used instead of a parting tool to face off the end of a blank. The skew will raise the hackles on your neck until you have made peace with it. When you have, it is amazing how simple it seems. Yet how difficult it was to learn! "EUREKA! I HAVE FOUND IT!"

Parting Tools

The parting tool is the easiest tool to use to cut a clean shoulder. (The skew can be used, but is more difficult.) The parting tool is a cutting tool, not a scraping tool. Start the cut high and advance in and down to meet the diameter and height of the tool at the center of the work piece. When you learn to make a parting cut, the results will astonish you with a clean and controlled cut.

Mandrels

One-piece Mandrel: A one piece mandrel, supported between the headstock and the tailstock, allows both blanks to be turned at the same time.

WARNING: If there is any misalignment between the headstock and the tailstock, the barrel will be malformed. Usually the barrel will have an oval or uneven diameter at the tailstock end. This condition gets worse as the distance from the headstock increases because the mandrel is being pulled to one side and out of alignment by the tailstock. In other words, a bow has been created--neither desirable nor tolerable!

Two-piece Mandrel: The two-piece mandrel is easier to load. One piece is normally held by a drill chuck in the headstock. The other half is inserted into the other end of the tube and supported by a 60º tip in a live center. These mandrels normally hold one tube at a time, but are also made as double barrel mandrels to hold two tubes.

The disadvantage to the two-piece mandrel is that there is no solid axis between the headstock and tailstock, which can result in a deflection at the center. With the double barrel mandrels, this deflection can contribute to an out of round condition at the center of the two barrels, especially if too much end pressure is applied. Excessive pressure applied to the work piece while cutting can produce the same problem.

Morse Taper Vs. Straight or Chuck Type Drive

The Morse taper has a positive repeatability. The straight or chuck type loses its ability to be rechucked in perfect alignment because the jaws of the chuck tend to mar the finished surface of the mandrel over time.

Alternative Mandrel

To create your own temporary mandrel, secure a dowel in a chuck and cut the diameter of the dowel to a press fit to the inside of the brass tube in the blank you are turning. This will create a concentric axis of the tube at the headstock. Using a 60º live center, with the lathe running, lightly bring up the tailstock, allow it to seek its center and lock down the tailstock. This will provide a true axis and concentric hold on the brass tube allowing you to turn the outside diameter that is needed.

Disassembly Kits

These kits are available for most pens and provide the necessary drivers and instructions to take pens apart to correct mistakes, faulty parts or any other gremlins that may attack a pen. It is money well spent and a necessity, unless you can walk on water.

Finishes

Buffing

Buffing with Tripoli or various rouges can produce flawless finishes on man-made materials as well as some other materials we may come upon. Buffing can also even out some of our other finishes.

Wax

I feel that wax is not a durable finish on its own. After I have assembled the pen, I do use wax to enhance the appearance and give a smooth, pleasing feel to the original finish.

French Polish

This is my favorite finish. It is one of the more durable finishes and develops a patina with time.

I apply it with the lathe running at the same speed as I turn, which is the maximum speed. It builds up a filled surface, unlike a lower speed which takes more time and gives less than satisfactory results—not my way. Additional coats should be buffed with 0000 steel wood to create a uniform finish.

Brushing Lacquer

Deft® is the one I prefer. It can be used like a French polish. It builds up a slow finish, even though the drying is fast when used this way. Surface rings or pick up can be removed with 0000 steel wool. The resulting finish is very durable, but is time consuming to produce.

Deft is also available in spray cans. Take the piece out of the lathe to avoid an unclean lathe. (I protect mine at all times when possible.) With repeated light coats and buffing with 0000 steel wool between applications, you can build a durable finish.

Glues

Cyanoacrylate

Wood turning and cyanoacrylate go hand in hand. It would be difficult to turn without them. They can fill cracks, bond pieces together, and repair surfaces. On some burl woods, I prefer to coat the inside of the blank hole with the thin cyanoacrylate before putting in the tube. This bonds hidden cracks, bark inclusions, or problems that may arise that I cannot see. I like to use the medium density to glue the tubes to the blanks and heavy density where more working time or gap filling qualities are needed. Thin cyanoacrylate can be used to strengthen punky or suspect wood and help build a quick finish in porous materials by flooding the surface with the glue and removing the excess when close to the finished diameter. A disadvantage to cyanoacrylate is that it becomes brittle with age.

Polyurethane

This glue is waterproof, cleans from the inside of tubes easily, expands to fill cracks, and provides a good bond to the brass tubes. The expanding properties of this glue also allow us to drill a slightly larger hole in our blank and still have a good bond to the tube. When I glue Corian, Dymondwood, antler, or very hard woods, I use this glue almost exclusively. To ensure a good bond, I use a q-tip to evenly coat the inside of the blank. I feel that using a slightly oversize hole with polyurethane glue that does not become brittle allows a small amount of movement or give. This helps prevent the blank from cracking as a result of temperature or humidity changes.

Epoxy: Two-Part

This epoxy provides good adhesion between wood and metal. It is user friendly as it can be used quickly or can provide extended working time. I prefer it for assembly because it can be wiped off without harming the finish. This is also a very good glue for gluing in the brass tubes.

White or Yellow Glue

I don't use these glues because they provide a poor bond between the metal and the wood. These glues can be used to laminate woods together prior to drilling.

Deft®

This finish can be used at assembly to create a bond between the tubes and the parts that is less substantial than that created by epoxy. It allows you to take pieces apart later, but still provides more security than pressed parts alone.

Drilling

Bullet Drill

My favorite drill. This drill cuts with less deflection than any I know of, is aggressive, but not overly aggressive, evacuates chips easily, and has a durable cutting edge. The main disadvantage is that the drill bits are sized from 1/16 to 1/2 inch by 64ths only. In pen making, number drills and metric drills provide a definite advantage. However, some of the decimal drills are close enough to the necessary size, and the expanding qualities of polyurethane glue will make the adjustment. I feel there is no equal to a bullet drill to drill angled Dymondwood.

Brad Point

This is a good drill and is available in the necessary metric sizes.

Parabolic

These are also made in the necessary metric as well as decimal sizes. They are good drills, but are very aggressive, and the work piece has a tendency to climb the drill as the bit breaks through the bottom surface, which can cause splitting or breakout.

Step Drills

Step drills are used for step tubes. To create a step drill, we select a drill with the correct major diameter and the other diameters are ground to their respective sizes. The area of the minor diameter has the flute clearance of the major diameter which does not allow adequate chip clearance for the minor diameter. When using these drills it is necessary to evacuate the chips more often than we normally would. One solution is to first drill a hole to the full depth for the minor diameter. Then use the step drill to complete the other diameter or diameters.

Chucking Reamers

Occasionally we will drill a hole which will deflect and bind when we insert the brass tube. We could either use an oversized drill or a reamer, which is much more rigid, to create a straight hole. Sometimes when blanks are drilled, but not used immediately, the holes may distort or warp. A reamer can correct this situation as well.

TIP: Occasionally we may have wood that is not totally dry and suitable for pen making. If we need it, one way to speed the drying process is to drill an undersized tube hole through the blank. This will allow for airflow through the blank, speeding the drying process. When the drying is complete, we redrill the hole to the proper diameter.

Arbor Press with Modifications

I use an arbor press, which was designed to work with metal, to assemble the pens, but I have made several modifications to adjust to the needs of softer materials. Both the ram, which is the top or driving portion, and the anvil must be covered with some material to protect the pen parts. Hardwood is normally used, but with continued use the wood deteriorates and gets dents and distortions. I prefer corian which is more durable and provides a more solid feel than wood, but does not mar the pen like metal.

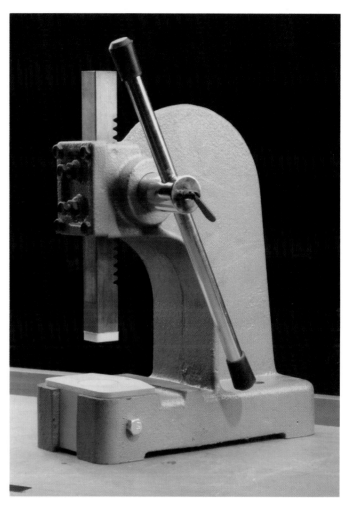

Corian attached to the ram.

I use a 1/4" piece of corian, cut to the shape of the ram and held in place with double stick tape.

Corian inserted into the hardwood block provides a durable working surface on the anvil. I drilled a hole into the hardwood block and used double-face taped to hold the corian in place.

To gain gap capacity I use a thin piece of hardwood to span the gap in the anvil of the press. This makes a flexible surface with a spongy feel.

Press blocks

I made these press blocks to press in parts that may have threads or some feature that could be damaged. These allow me to apply the pressure to the shoulder. This requires a clearance hole large enough to let the endangered part slide through but still contact the shoulder and deep enough to prevent the endangered part from hitting the anvil. You will need to develop blocks sized to fit a variety of conditions.

By fitting a piece of hard maple into the clearance area under the ram and cross pinning it by drilling and tapping for a 3/8" bolt, I have established a more than adequate surface to seat pens with a solid feel. The left side has been tapped. The other walls and the wooden block were drilled 3/8" with the block in place so the bolt and block fit tightly with no give.

Dymondwood Project

Dymondwood is made in straight strips which can be purchased 1/2" to 5/8" thick, 1 and 1/4" to 2 and 1/2 " wide and about 4' long. The precise measurements vary between vendors and lots. The normal pen would have straight lines, parallel to the axis of the pen. We can produce diagonal stripes by cutting and gluing the strip, creating a different, and very attractive design.

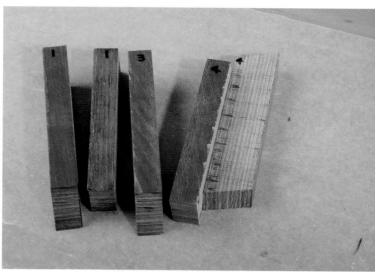

The strip will need to be cut into parallelograms. The angle for the end cuts can vary, but 73º or something close to it makes a nice pattern. The X dimension establishes the length of the finished blank.

If the pieces are aligned correctly, the color sequence for this particular pattern will be red, green, red, green. If a piece is reversed, two reds or two greens will be next to each other, creating a mis-match of the plies which will show up in the finished product. Some mis-matches are much more pronounced than others, but care can avoid any mis-match.

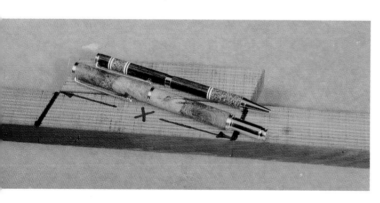

A standard blank length, purchased already cut, is 5 inches. If you are only making standard straight twist pens, you can reduce the X-dimension to 4 1/2 inches. If you are turning various styles of pens, extend the X dimension to provide sufficient stock for your longest style. I feel it is better to have excess than to be too frugal and limit your choice of styles.

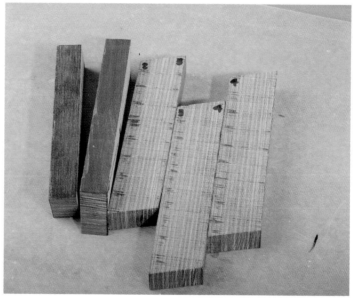

As you cut the pieces, lay them next to each other, maintaining them in the order they were cut, and number them. This helps lessen the impact of any deviation in the colors and keeps the plies in proper alignment or sequence. I use a band saw and a miter gage to cut my angles, and a fence to establish and control the X-dimension.

Use a stationary belt sander, to lightly abrade the mating surfaces for better adhesion when gluing. Don't change the angle or sand off any stock--just a light roughing-up.

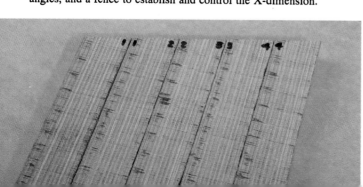

TIP: Place wax paper on your work surface as no glue will adhere to it.

Apply a generous amount of glue to one surface

Now that the segments are glued together, we must lay out one more cut. This is the same line as the X-dimension, from top left corner to bottom right corner of the end segment. Cut the end segment along the line drawn.

and rub the mating surfaces together to spread the glue evenly. I use the heaviest cyanoacrylate because it fills gaps better and gives me a longer time to work.

Move the triangle you have removed to the other side, maintaining the red to green glue surface match and glue it. The parallelogram has now become a rectangle.

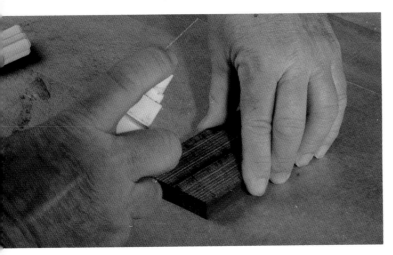

Lay them flat on the paper, align the ends and hold the joint together, giving a shot of accelerator to cure the joint. Continue to glue the segments together in their numbered sequence.

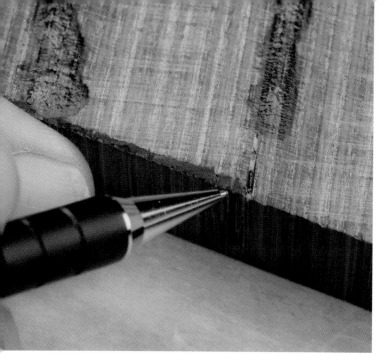

Sometimes the edges of the segments are chipped or damaged in some way so they do not fit perfectly. This one has a ply damaged on the end, resulting in a small, but significant gap. The gap may be turned out so that it does not affect the finished pen, but better be safe than sorry--fix it now. Occasionally some of the plies in the stock itself are not bonded. Check and glue if necessary.

Using a belt sander, knock off any excessive glue to allow the piece to lie flat while you cut the blanks. Now is a good time to recheck the joint lines to make sure there are no voids. If there are fill them with glue and re-sand.

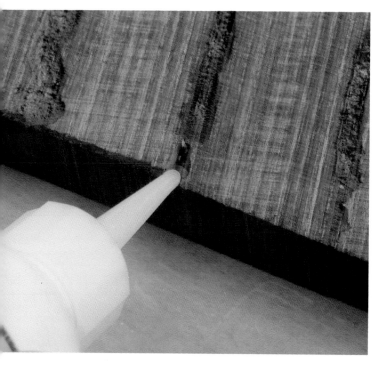

Using the medium density cyanoacrylate, I fill the gap. The medium density which has thinner viscosity, penetrates better, but still has enough body to fill the void. Turn the glued segments over and look for cracks or gaps on the other side. If there are minute cracks, flood these areas with the thin cyanoacrylate which penetrates deeper than the other two glues. Larger voids may need medium density to fill them. Hit with accelerator to assure that the glues are cured.

Set up a fence on the saw to the same thickness as the glued stock. This will produce square pen blanks. The picture shows two blanks next to the rectangle in their natural position. The two blanks to the left are rotated 90 degrees.

Click Pen

This style pen is my personal favorite. It can be operated with one hand, has a mechanism that is reliable, and works well. It is slightly larger than the standard twist pen, accepts the same refills used for Parker® pens, and has a pleasant appearance. For this pen, I will use the Dymondwood blanks made previously.

Clamp the blank into the vee-block with a hand clamp. This makes a very solid set-up that is easy to move. Always put the blank in the vee-block with the center section up to be drilled first. If there is any deflection, it is away from the joint. This helps to keep grain mis-alignment to a minimum at the center joint, making a better looking grain match. Note our mark is on the right hand side of the vee-block.

Cut two sections from one of the blanks to fit the barrel lengths, with a little extra to allow for trimming. I always mark the center of both blanks so I have no problem aligning grain pattern at any time.

Center the blank under the drill chuck with a pointer for the first blank and lock down. This pen calls for an 8 mm, but I use a size O drill to allow more clearance for the brass tube. Remove the pointer and install the drill.

Bring down your drill and allow it to seek its center before applying pressure. Slowly advance the drill until the flutes have entered the work.

For drilling I use a compound table for ease of set-up. The table is not necessary, but it is a nice luxury. I have clamped a vee-block with a piece of particle board of uniform thickness beneath it to protect the table. (The vee-block can be clamped to the drill press table instead.)

When drilling, do not apply too much pressure, but apply enough to allow the drill to cut freely. You will be able to feel this cutting action with experience. Evacuate chips often.

TIP: After drilling, the brass tube should slide freely into the hole for the entire length. any binding can cause cracking after the pen has been completed. Re-drill or use a chucking reamer to eliminate any binding. This could save you heartbreak 6 months later.

Put the other half of the blank in the vee-block, center up and the mark to the left hand side of the vee-block, clamp

and drill. We reverse the marks in the vee-block from top to bottom blank to set up on two common surfaces. Even if the hole is drilled slightly off center, it will be in the same direction for both pieces.

Now that the glue has dried and the blanks are trimmed with the pen mill, we can mount them on the mandrel, using the proper bushings for the pen. Note the alignment marks on the centers of the blanks.

Cutting angled dymondwood presents some problems. Dymondwood is brittle, and since we have created an angular pattern, we are always cutting against the grain on half the blank. With each rotation of the blank the cut shifts from end grain to face grain. When turning against the grain (end grain) we have a tendency to lift the plies and chip them off. Going with the grain presents no special problems.

When I reduce the blank to a cylinder, I use a straight on cut with a spindle gouge. This can still result in minor surface tearing, but as long as I do not go below the finished diameter, I can still do the finish cuts. No matter which tool is used, gouge or skew, angular cut dymondwood demands a light touch and cut. A skew will work, but it has a greater tendency to get under the plies and do greater damage than the gouge.

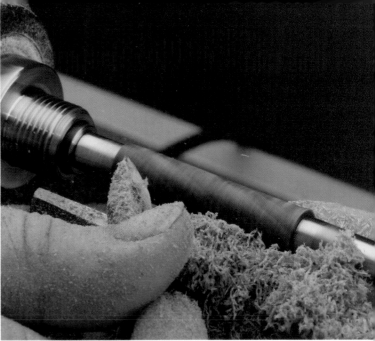

That shaving at the tip of the gouge is the key to success. The shear cut requires real concentration. Do not ride the bevel on this cut. The angle of the tool in relation to the axis of the lathe is most important. With a curved cutting edge on the gouge, this angle changes constantly as you move down the blank. The key is to find a sweet spot and maintain it. A light cut is required, because you do not want to remove too much material with the cut. If the cut is too heavy, you risk a rough cut with a less than perfect surface. The cut I have described will leave a smoother surface than any cut I know, especially on angled dymondwood. The disadvantage to the cut is that not riding a bevel demands a high level of coordination and concentration to cut an even plane without bumps, dips, etc.

> **TIP**: To find the sweet spot, stop the lathe, and rotate it by hand while moving your gouge to find the perfect angle. When you have, learn to maintain it with the lathe running. Practice. Rome was not built in a day. As you build your skill level and understanding of the cut, it is possible to cut back and forth with the same edge in both directions.

As you near the final diameter, change from a straight on cut to a shear cut. The shear cut is made by standing the gouge on its side and cutting without really using the bevel. Support the piece with your fingers and hold the gouge to the tool rest with your thumb to minimize chatter. The touch really needs to be light. Understand mistakes are made. Please do not hold me responsible for yours during your learning period. I lived hard during mine.

Misconception: most people call it a shear scrape. These small shavings are a result of a shear cut and not a scrape.

In order to show you what can go wrong and how to fix it, I have shown a blank with mistakes while the blank is still oversize for photographic purposes. Normally, this repair would be done at the finishing stage when the blank is reduced to its proper diameter. The roughness is extreme, also to highlight the conditions which you might encounter, or cause.

The pits and tears are caused by poor tool control. At the finished diameter, these faults would be too deep to be removed by sanding. Another problem which may require the same repair is the small voids that sometimes occur when the plies are not bonded to each other.

It is easier to allow some of the drying to occur on its own before using accelerator. Use caution with the accelerator because it will sometimes leave a white residue from curing too rapidly. I do not fill the voids with dust because the multi-colored laminations makes matching virtually impossible.

Flood the blank with the thin cyanoacrylate

Using a light sheer cut, cut the excess glue from the surface.

and, rotating the lathe by hand, even out with a piece of polyurethane packing material. If the defects are severe, you could use the medium density which will help fill chip outs, torn grain, and build up a thicker coat.

Stop and look to see if you have filled your voids. If not reapply glue.

TIP: When applying glue, be careful not to glue the blank to the bushings. If you occasionally apply a light coat of oil to the mandrel and bushings, it will help keep the glue from adhering. I use tung oil finish because it dries on the parts without leaving a reside as machine oil would.

There's a void, but it is small enough to sand out.

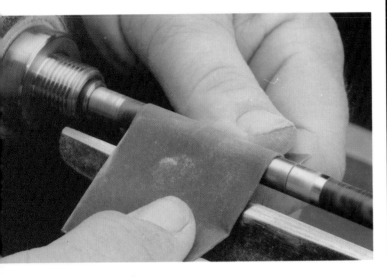

Sand the pen with 180 to 400 grain and finish. Sanding with the grain will help eliminate rings.

The composition of dymondwood contains its own finish. To remove minor scratches and imperfections, I use a concentric sewn cloth wheel charged with Tripoli on a buffer.

The glue is so compatible with this material which already has a lot of glue, that this type of repair is virtually blemish free. There is no need to give up on a blank that still has enough material to maintain the necessary diameter.

When buffing the piece hold it at an angle, rather than 90º to the wheel, which will help eliminate any sanding imperfections.

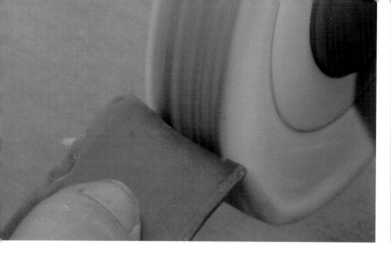

Move to the loose-sewn cloth wheel on the other side of the buffer. This side is charged with wax

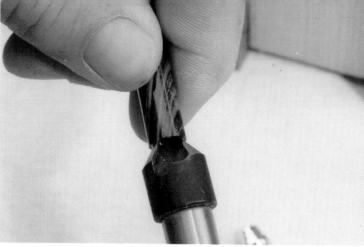

Chamfer the inside of the tube to make sure that there is no interference between the metal parts and the tube. This will ensure a tight fit between the wood and the metal fittings.

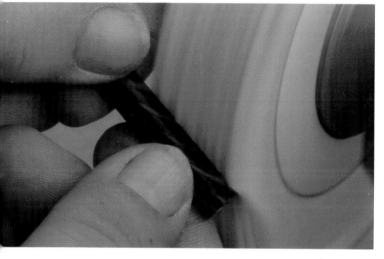

to create the final lustrous finish, with a nice feel.

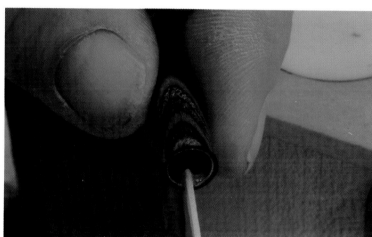

Apply a small amount of epoxy to the inside of the bottom tube with a toothpick.

TIP: I use a 2-part epoxy to glue any joint that has threads so that the twisting motion of the threads does not cause the fitting to move. I use epoxy because it is user friendly with more working time, excess can be wiped off without damaging the finish, and it provides a good bond to metal.

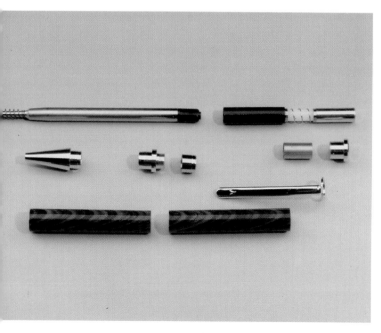

This is the layout of parts for the assembly of our click pen.

Assemble the two threaded, center bushings and insert the gold end into the bottom barrel.

Then using a wooden block with a clearance hole for the threads, push against the shoulder of the fitting, and press home. By pressing against the shoulder you do not take a chance of damaging the threads.

Undo the center joint. Insert the tip into the bottom barrel and use the pressing block to seat in order not to damage the threads on the center connector.

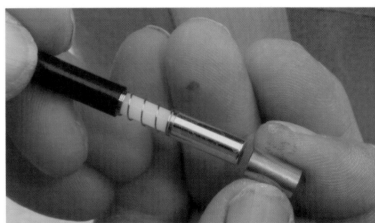

Put glue into the top half of the barrel, insert the center bushing, align the grain,

Insert the small tube over the top of the transmission.

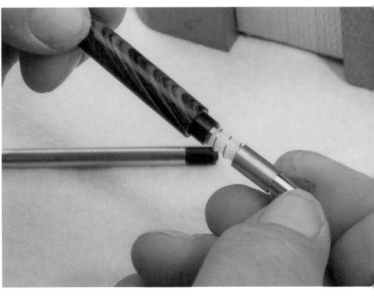

and seat the two. This procedure will ensure that the grain alignment for the two halves of the pen will match when the pen is assembled.,

Put the transmission into the top tube

And the clip and retainer over the top of the transmission.

Seat the cap.

Use a pressing block sized for the clip cap to make sure that you push against the cap and not the transmission.

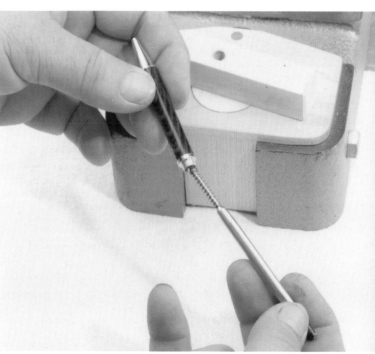

Insert the refill.

Put the pen together.

Follow the same basic steps to turn and finish the pencil.

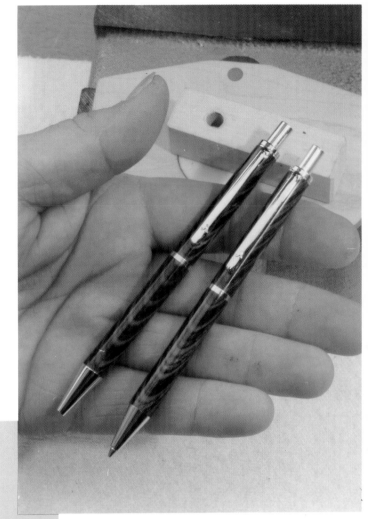

Pen and pencil set finished.

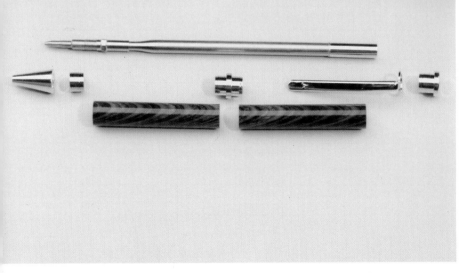

The layout for the pencil.

Antler Pen

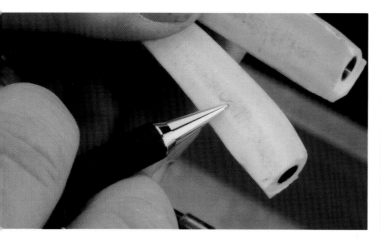

When using antler, the color and texture of the finished pen will be determined by the way the blank was cut or the part of the antler from which it was taken. This beam was split. I am pointing to the heart of the antler which will be more porous than the rest of the blank.

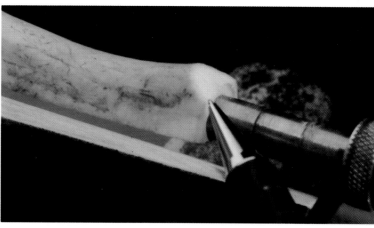

Sometimes the antlers are so out of shape that you need to trim the corners to allow you to get your tool rest close to your work. Be careful that you do not remove stock below the bushing diameter when you trim.

This blank was cut from the end of the tine. It is almost solid bone, with very little porosity, which will result in a much denser, lighter colored pen.

I prefer to use a 3/8 inch spindle gouge to rough down the blank.

Normally the blank is completely out of balance and will cause catches so a light touch is necessary.

Mount the glued and trimmed blanks onto the mandrel.

Continue to reduce the blanks until you start to near the diameter of the bushings.

Stop the lathe and examine the blank for porous spots. This one has very little porous material, which is an exception. Some have an almost completely porous surface.

Examine the porous areas to see if any of the brass tube is showing through. If it is, take some of the antler dust and work it into the pores to hide the tube.

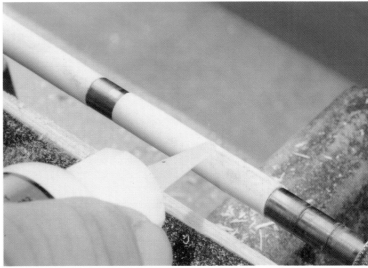

Reduce the diameter

Using the thin cyanoacrylate (superglue), saturate the porous areas.

to approximately .015 above the finished diameter.

Before the glue sets up, while rotating the lathe by hand, spread the glue uniformly over the piece. I use a piece of polyurethane packing material because it absorbs less of the glue than do most other materials, so it is less likely to adhere to the piece while I work.

Hit the blank with accelerator to cure the glue.

Note: Be careful not to get the glue on you while you work. No one and nothing totally escapes superglue.

Lightly remove the glue from the surface. This should still leave the pores filled. If any voids or bad spots remain, re-coat and repeat the process.

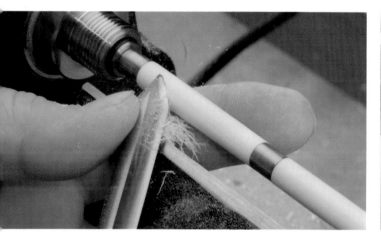

Standing the gouge on its side, use a shear cut to make a finished cut across the blank. A skew will work, but I can take a lighter cut using the gouge with a shear cut. Note the fine shavings. This is not a scrape.

Sand. I normally start at 180, and progress through 600 grit. At this point I move to a buffer and use cloth wheels with Tripoli. The last step is a coat of wax. The antler is dense enough to achieve a finish of its own and does not need an applied finish.

I am within .005 of my finished diameter.

Use the medium density cyanoacrylate to re-coat the blanks to seal any pores that may have reappeared. Hit with accelerator and cure.

Finished antler pen. The barrel below is also antler, but cut more from the center including the marrow which gives it the red color. The marrow, however, is much more porous and requires more filling and care.

Corian Dymondwood
Combination

I am using a standard 7mm twist pen.

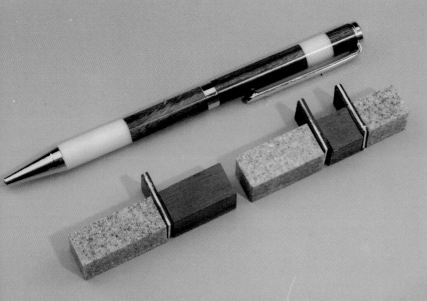

Rough up the pickguard surface with a fine grit paper to assure a good bond.

The materials for the Corian Dymondwood pen laid out in sequence with one of our original examples next to it. The different materials and sequence will create a pen that is similar in style, but will look completely different. I am using a flecked pattern corian and a color of dymondwood which is compatible with the corian. I am reversing the corian and dymondwood from the example pen. Finally, I have added pickguard to create a distinct separation between the other materials. The materials for the Corian Dymondwood pen have been rough cut to provide my pattern, and will be finish trimmed after they have been glued together. The Corian is generally 1/2" thick, so I make both dymondwood and Corian blanks 1/2" square to create uniform set-up. I leave extra material on one side of the pickguard material to facilitate handling during gluing.

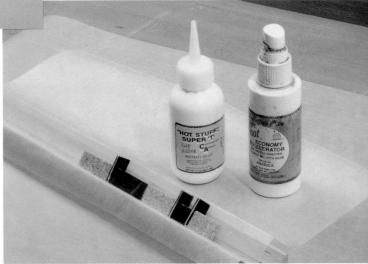

Put wax paper in the vee-block and set the pieces in the proper sequence or order, ready for gluing.

This is a jig I made to help simplify the gluing operation. It keeps the blanks aligned and out of trouble. The jig is merely a piece of wood with two 45 degree angles to form a vee-block.

Apply a liberal amount of medium-density cyanoacrylate to the both sides of the pickguard

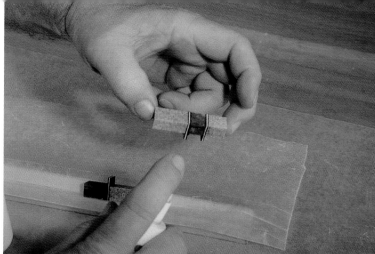

drop it between its mating two surfaces. Press the pieces down into the vee-block to assure proper alignment

Remove pieces from the vee-block and apply accelerator to the two sides that were in the vee-block.

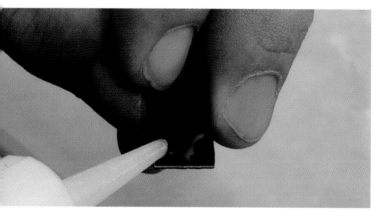

And immediately do the same to the next joint.

I have trimmed the excess pickguard material with a band saw, trimmed the blanks to the proper length for the brass tube, leaving a small amount for squaring, drilled holes for the brass tubes, glued the tube in that hole, and squared the ends with a pen mill. Marking the center for alignment is not needed on this pen as the difference in top and bottom is quite apparent.

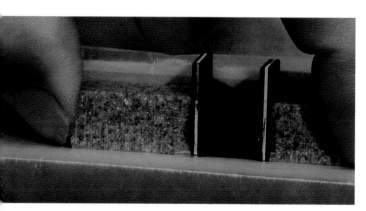

Making sure all the pieces are nested in the vee-block,

Apply accelerator.

WARNING: The melting point for pickguard material is fairly low. Corian and Dymondwood create a lot of heat during drilling, and, if care is not taken, the pickguard material will melt on the inside of the blank and it will loose its color definition.

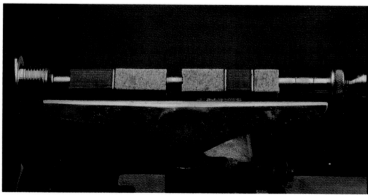

Mount on the lathe using standard straight pen bushings.

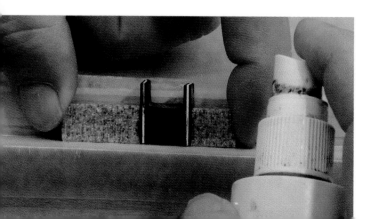

Using a spindle gouge and a straight on cut, reduce the blank till you approach the bushing diameter. When working with a combination of materials, the different densities of the materials will cut differently. When cutting from a hard material to a softer material, the tool tends to cut more aggressively when it hits the soft material and could create an undercut condition. We must be aware of this and adjust pressure as we go.

Since the materials are of different consistencies there is a real possibility that you will have an uneven surface. To help even the surface, you can use a sanding block to reduce the high spots.

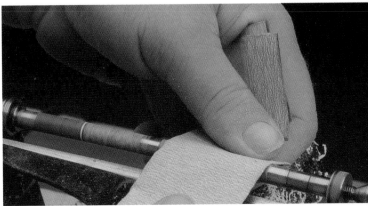

As we approach the bushing diameter, a skew can be used to make a more uniform cut between the different materials.

After the sanding block, sand as usual. I normally work with silicone carbide paper from 180 grit to 400 grit. This paper is white and does not leave a visible residue in the pores of light colored woods as would the dark wet and dry paper. Since these materials have no pores, I use a 600 grit wet and dry for an even smoother surface.

Reduce the blank

to the bushing diameter.

The finished pen next to the example pen. So much alike and yet so different!

Tagua Nut Accent

We are always looking for a new place to decorate the pen or put an initial, something that will make it special. In this pen we are adding a pattern of round tagua nut dots for contrast. We need a pen such as the roller ball pen with sufficient diameter to accommodate the dots. The wood is dark Cocobolo.

Tip: On the bottom of the cap of this type rollerball is exposed end grain. Before the final finish, coat the end grain with cyanoacrylate to add strength. Lightly re-trim this area, and finish as usual.

Use a scratch awl and the tool rest to scribe a line down the blank. This will be our center line for the series of dots. Now remove the barrel from the mandrel.

Cut and drill the blanks. Do not glue the brass tubes into the blanks. Gluing will be done after our inlaying is complete. Place the loose brass tubes into the blanks and mount on the mandrel. Even though the brass tubes are loose, they will still hold the blanks concentric to the mandrel.

I am only turning the top blank now because that is the only barrel I am decorating. Turn the barrel a constant diameter, as we need the outer surface parallel to the hole in the blank.

Tagua nuts are also called "vegetable ivory." They are hard, a legal ivory substitute, and readily available. They also have a void and or discoloration in the center of the nut, which we can work around. Cut a section lengthwise from the nut large enough to accommodate the size dot that you want with a bandsaw.

Saturate the outside of the blank with superglue to make sure there are no cracks. Use care not to glue the tube into the blank.

I mount a wooden dowel in a drill chuck into the headstock. This will be the drive for the nut. I use a small live center with a small hardwood cup center in the tailstock so there is less drag, and therefore less chance of cracking a small diameter during start-up. Trim the ends of the nut section so they will match the ends of the dowel and your live center.

Face off the end of the dowel and put the nut between the dowel and the live center. Balance out to make sure you have stock. Lightly tighten to hold it, and apply cyanoacrylate to the dowel and nut. Hit with accelerator. It is now firmly attached.

With a parting tool remove the tagua nut.

Reduce the tagua nut. Gently take it down to whatever diameter you need.

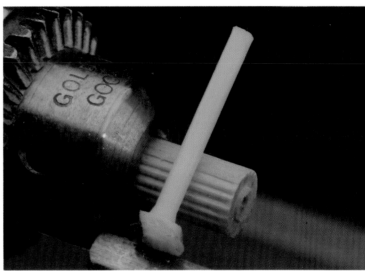

This tagua nut piece is ready for the next step.

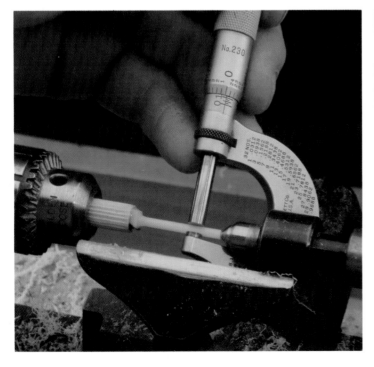

I use a micrometer to ensure my dimensions are precise. This one is the small one: 1/8" diameter.

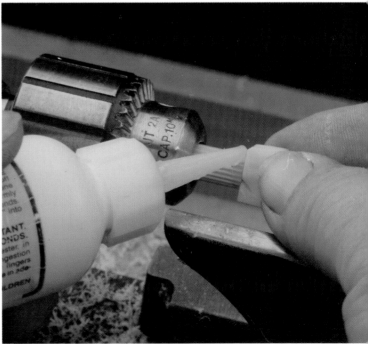

You can also use small chips or pieces of slabs to create individual plugs. Just glue the piece on the end of the dowel,

and turn.

Remove the brass tube from the barrel, put the barrel in the vee-block and drill. The diameter of the plugs should stay within the diameter of the hole in the barrel. Our first hole is 3/8".

This one is 1/4".

Insert a matching tagua nut plug. Using the scribe line, drill the hole for the second plug.

At the drill press, use a vee-block made from a piece of scrap. Center and clamp the block by locating the exact center of the vee under the chuck. This will allow our blank to lay in the vee and be drilled right down the center line.

Continue to drill the holes and insert the plugs.

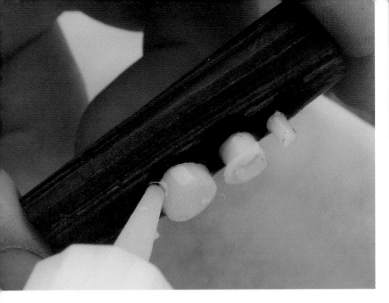

Glue the nuts with the thin cyanoacrylate

Carefully work down each plug.

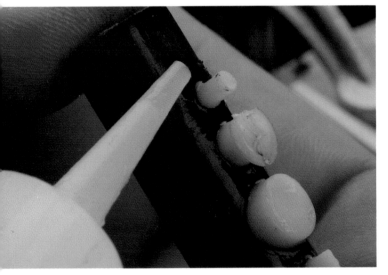

making sure all mating surfaces are saturated. Spray on accelerator.

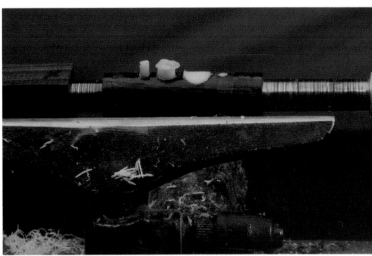

It is best to concentrate on one plug at a time.

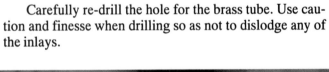

Carefully re-drill the hole for the brass tube. Use caution and finesse when drilling so as not to dislodge any of the inlays.

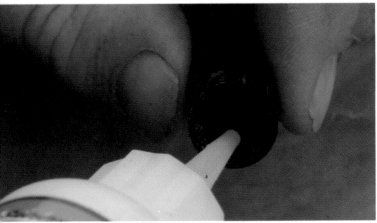

Glue the brass tubes into the blanks. Trim the ends with a pen mill and mount that porcupine on the mandrel.

Reduce the excess plugs down to the barrel diameter. Now that you are down to the barrel diameter, there is less chance that the plugs will chip out because they are bonded all the way around.

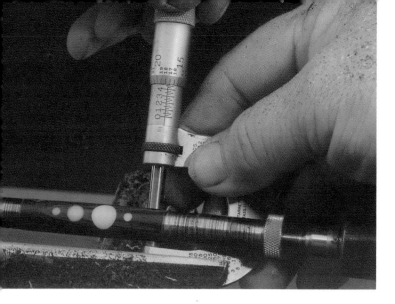

It is reduced it to the desired diameter

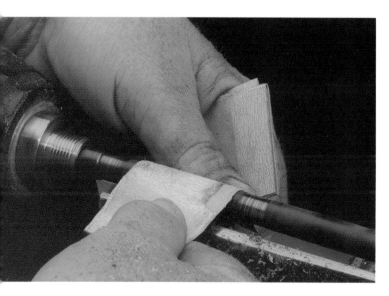

and ready to sand, and finish.

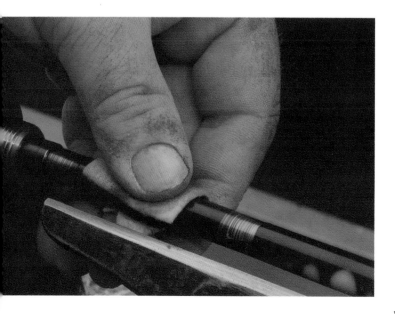

I use a French polish for a finish. If you get pick-up rings, you can level them off with 0000 steel wool.

When we started this pen, we mentioned that you do not want to have a plug that is larger than the inside diameter of the hole for the tube. The large plug in this pen is right at the limit. As you can see, it has become elliptical on the sides, while the smaller holes still retain a round shape.

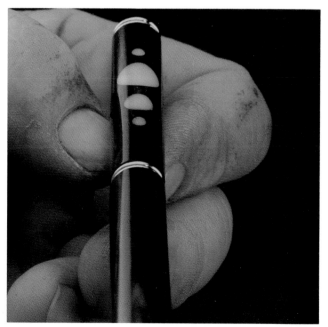

Notice how, having used our scribed center line for the set-up, our holes are in alignment. The ellipses on the large hole are even, showing that it is exactly centered.

Americana Pen

This is a new style pen that assembles and operates a little differently than any of the others. The pen blanks are shorter which allows you to use some of that stash of wood pieces that are too short for other styles, but too showy to throw out. I am using Black Ash burl.

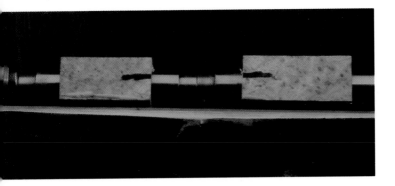

Drill, glue, and trim the pieces and mount them on the mandrel using the proper bushings.

Reduce the pen to the bushing diameters.

The pen is reduced and ready to sand.

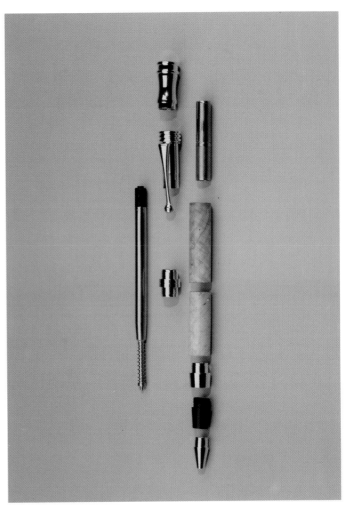

The layout for the Americana pen.

Using a press block to avoid damage to the threads, press the gold and black tips together.

Press the threaded tip coupler into the tip end of the bottom barrel.

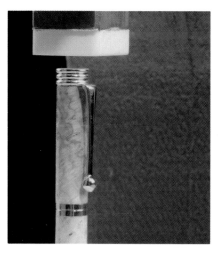

Making sure the grain is aligned, put the top and bottom barrel together with the center coupler.

Press the clip and twist mechanism coupler into the top of the long tube.

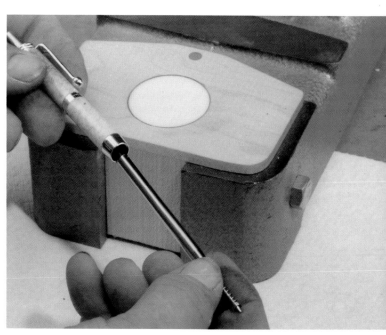

Slide the refill and spring into the tip end and screw on the tip assembly. Slide the cap over the twist mechanism.

Press the brass end of the twist mechanism in the twist mechanism coupler. Stop at 4 inches. If you seat it too deeply the refill will not retract, not deeply enough, it will not extend far enough. I have a vee-stop-block to help establish the proper depth. Mine is 3 and 7/8 inches. Start at 4" and keep trimming until you establish the length that works for you.

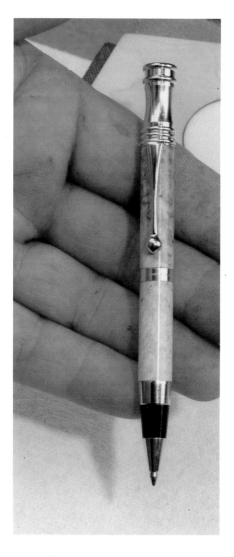

The completed pen. Go write.

Classic Rollerball Pen

A straight brass tube of the size required to accomodate the hardware necessary for making this pen (writing tip, refill, etc.) would make a less than graceful pen. By using brass stepped tubes, it is possible to taper the ends with flowing lines becasue of the reduced inside diameters. Hence, an eye appealing, comfortable pen. You will need to use different sized drills or a stepped drills to prepare the blank for the brass tube. We are using the stepped drills that are made to accompany this kit.

I used Eucalyptus burl for the pen.

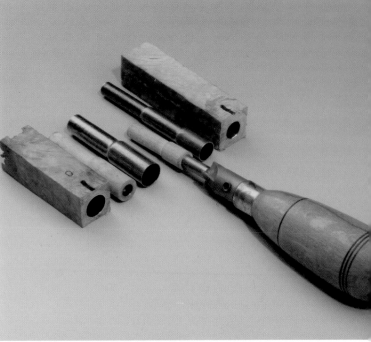

The shaft of the pen mill is a standard 7 mm diameter. This diameter is only good at the bottom end of the long tube. The other three diameters are too large to hold the mill in alignment. Using extra 7 mm brass tubes with the addition of sufficient hard maple glued to it, I have created internal stepped bushings.

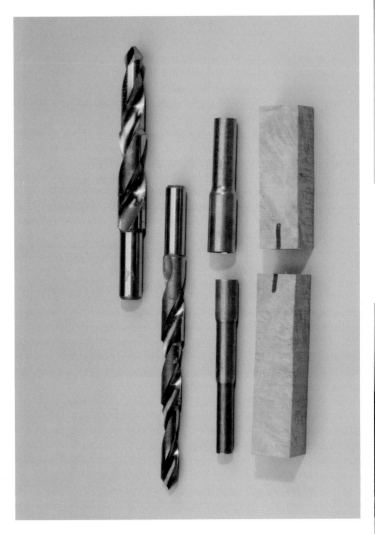

Note the way the tubes and stepped drills decrease in size. Be careful not to drill too deep. If you do, you may leave a void between the shoulder of the step and the brass tube which could cause breakthrough due to lack of material.

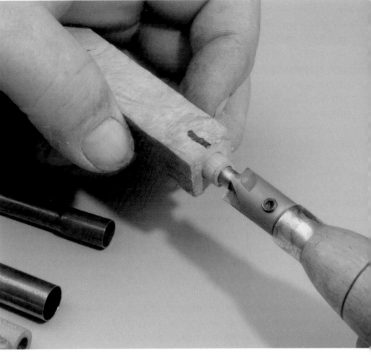

These bushings hold the pen mill concentric to the stepped tube for a clean, square trim. Trimming could be accomplished by using a skew during turning, but this provides a more acceptable end for the average individual.

Glue in the tubes. If using polyurethane glue, be aware of its expanding qualities. It has the tendency to swell against the shoulders and push the brass tube out of the blank. I use a rubber band around the blank legthwise to act as a clamp. Trim the ends, and mount the blanks onto the mandrel using the proper bushings.

Sand and finish the pen barrels. Then move the top barrel from its position at the headstock to the tailstock end. I have added extra bushings to extend the barrel past the end of the mandrel.

Turn as usual.

This allows me to use the 60º center on the live center with a clearance to turn a 1/16th relief without damaging my bushings.

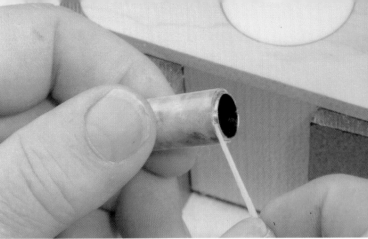

In order to provide a tight uniform fit for the center trim bushing, this 1/16th relief needs to be a concentric cut.

Put a little epoxy on the brass tube and shoulder.

Precise.

Press the center trim band onto the tube.

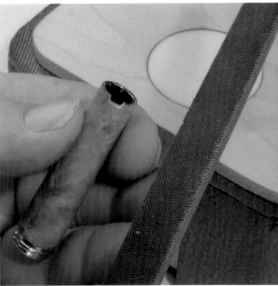

The parts laid out for the Classic Rollerball pen.

File a notch with a 6 inch bastard file to make space for the clip so the cap will nest to the top of the barrel.

Apply a little epoxy to the inside of the barrel

and seat the cap clip assembly.

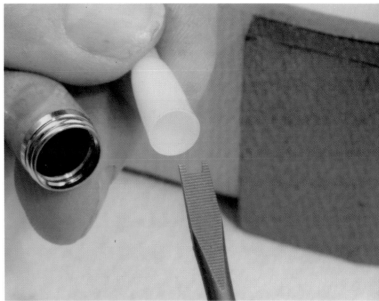

Insert the white plastic closing cap and screw onto the end of the clip assembly. I use a screw driver with a notch filed in it with clearance for the screwed stud on the cap. This allows me to adjust the closing cap securely without interference from the length of the stud. Cap adjusting tools are available.

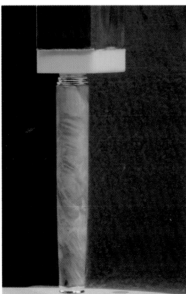

Press in the end cap. I put a little epoxy on the inside of the tube before seating the nib coupler because it provides a secure grip on a threaded insert.

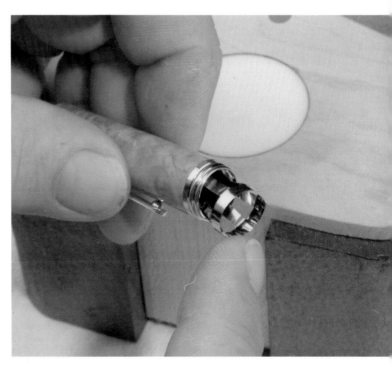

Roll up the nib spring and slide into the cap. This spring provides a means of holding the cap onto the bottom barrel during writing.

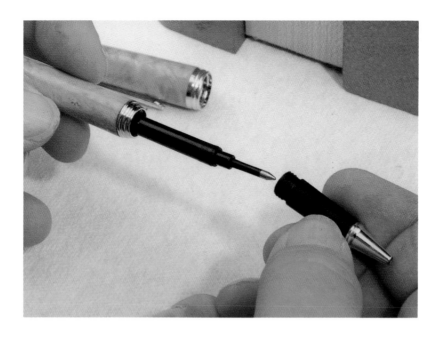

Assemble the two halves of the nib, drop the spring into the bottom barrel, put in the refill, screw in the nib assembly,

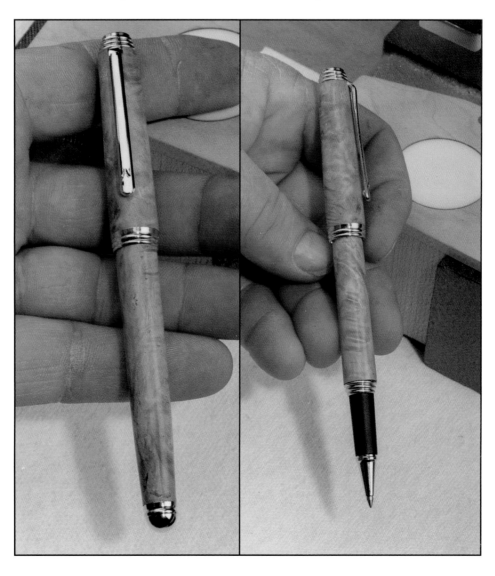

adjust the closing cap so the two barrels fit properly, and we have a completed pen.

Combination Pen/Pencil

At some point you may end up with a kit with no mandrel, no bushings, and no instructions. Or you may want to try something special and do not want to invest in bushings until you know you have something you want to repeat.

This project is a new pen/pencil combination housed in one barrel. Rotating the cap clockwise produces a pen, counter clockwise a pencil. In this exercise, we will work out problems I had because I received nothing but the parts. I will create a temporary mandrel to hold and turn the pen/pencil. For this pen I will use Thuya burl.

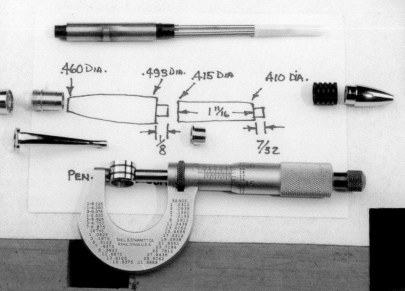

Make a basic sketch and use a micrometer to check the diameter of the pieces that must be installed at the ends of each tube. Mark the diameters and check to see if the shoulders need to be cut for things such as the center trim band. In this case the tip end of the bottom barrel does need a special cut. This sketch becomes the blue print to follow.

This particular pen has two different tube diameters. The top barrel is larger than the bottom. I have drilled my blanks, glued in the brass, but have not trimmed them. I will do the trimming as I work.

I put a drill chuck with a 3/8" dowel in the headstock, and a live center with a 60 degree tip. This will be the mandrel. Starting with the top barrel as it has the larger diameter, turn the dowel to the inside diameter of the brass tube. The fit should be snug as this will provide the means to drive the blank.

Bring up the tailstock and put the 60 degree center into the other end of the tube. Between the dowel and the tailstock we have now established a plane concentric to the axis of the lathe.

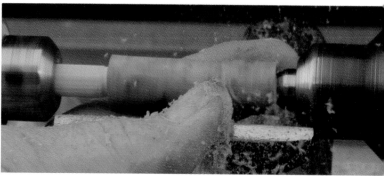

Start reducing the diameter of the blank.

Cut carefully and check often to make sure that you do not go below the diameters in the blueprint.

The shoulder length is derived by measuring the inside of the center trim band. I coated the measured area with black ink to make it clear in the photograph. The shoulder is 1/8".

We have reached the diameter plus a few thousandths for sanding. The dimension must be taken on the bottom of the top barrel, where the trim ring mates. A shoulder will be cut at that point.

Cut the 1/8" shoulder to the brass tube at the bottom end of the barrel.

Sand and finish the top tube. To trim the top of the tube, take a small parting tool and align yourself to get a nice clean 90 degree cut to the end of the brass tube.

If you sand and finish the barrel before doing these cuts, the corners will be sharp and defined, rather than rounded from the sanding.

The top barrel is turned.

Because the bottom barrel has a smaller diameter than the top, you will need to shave some of the diameter off the dowel to fit.

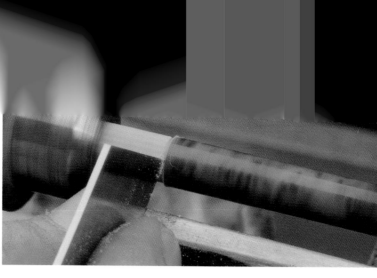

When the bottom barrel is turned, sanded, and finished make the cut to finish the top of the tube.

The bottom barrel is ready to turn.

Next trim the bottom of the tube. I cut a 7/32nds shoulder for the trim ring at the bottom of the tube.

Turn the bottom barrel as usual.

This again I derived by measuring the inside of the trim.

The edge of this tube is faced off precisely.

Push the shoulder on the bottom barrel into the trim ring.

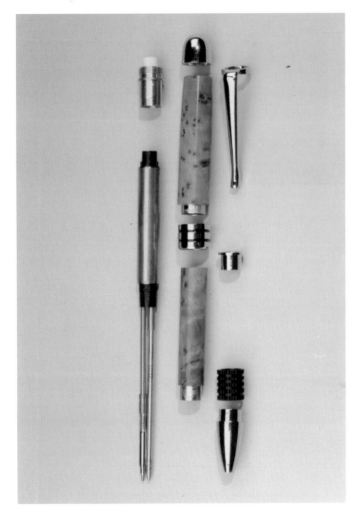

The parts for the combination pen/pencil.

Press the threaded insert into the top of the bottom barrel.

Put the tip into the black trim ring.

Put a little epoxy onto the brass tube and seat the center trim band on the tube against the wood shoulder.

Put a light coat of epoxy on the inside of the top tube, seat the clip and cap holder.

Slide the cap over the transmission and rotate clockwise for a pen,

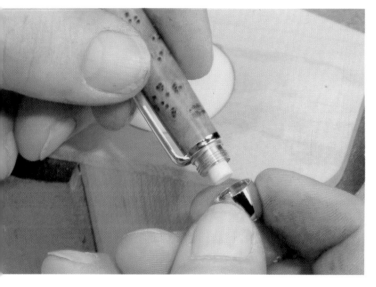

Add the eraser and cap.

and counterclockwise for a pencil.

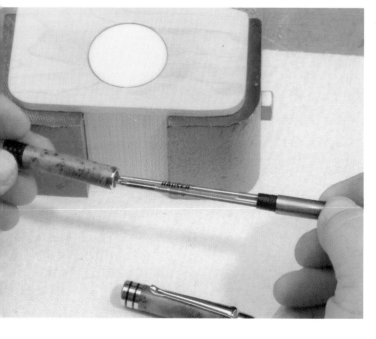

Screw in the pen/pencil transmission assembly.

The completed pen.

Father Sing's Pen

Every so often you want to do something different. You want to create something that reflects your own personality. This is my effort. I wanted to keep it a relatively small diameter, especially at the writing end. I also wanted to change the shape of the entire pen.

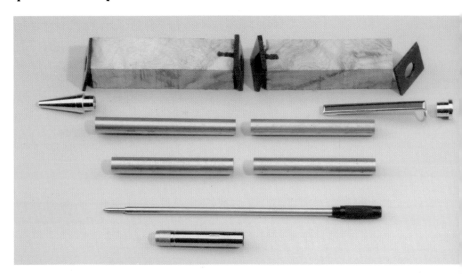

I used European style 7mm brass tubes. This style uses a longer tube on the bottom than on the top, creating an off-set look at the center rings. Notice the difference in the two 7mm tubes in front which I am not using. They are of equal length for the standard twist pen. The tip, transmission, refill, end clip cap, and a black-lined clip are from the standard twist pen. I am using pickguard material to create my own center bands and to accent each end. The wood is oak burl.

Drill, glue, trim the ends with the pen mill and mount the blanks on the lathe with standard bushings on the ends.

Replace the mandrel with a drill chuck. Insert half a two piece mandrel into the drill chuck. Continue to use the live center with the 60 degree tip in the tailstock. Now mount the barrel on the mandrel and bring up the tailstock.

Rough out the blanks

to approximate desired shape.

With a thin parting tool, cut a 1/16th shoulder to the brass tube on the top of the cap for a piece of 1/16th pickguard to provide an accent.

On the other end, cut a shoulder 3/32nds to the brass tube to accommodate half of the center ring.

Repeat the same process on the bottom barrel, making sure you put the 1/16th on the tip end and the 3/32nd on the center.

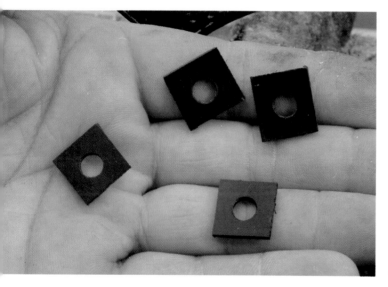

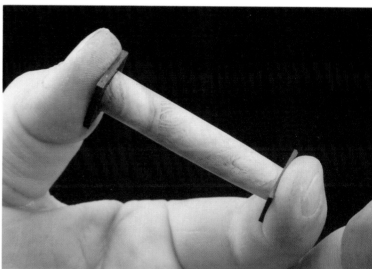

All four pieces of pickguard material need 7 mm holes drilled in their centers.

Check the pickguard for fit and you are ready to glue. The reason that I cut these on the lathe, rather than gluing them to the ends of the blank before turning, is so that they will end up concentric and a uniform thickness.

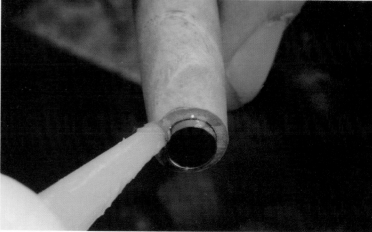

Remove the blank from the mandrel and put the pieces of pickguard on their respective ends to make sure that they fit flush with the brass tubes.

Put an adequate amount of medium density glue around the shoulder and rotate the pickguard material on to it.

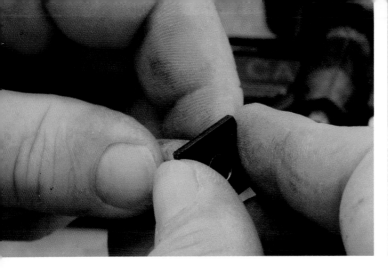 

Hold it flat and hit with accelerator. Repeat on the other end using the proper size pickguard.

Remount on the original mandrel using the standard twist pen bushings. The center bushing is used solely to separate the two barrels, as I am changing this dimension.

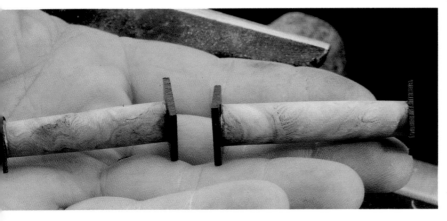 

Finish gluing the pickguard onto both barrels.

Work the pickguard material down to the diameter of the wood.

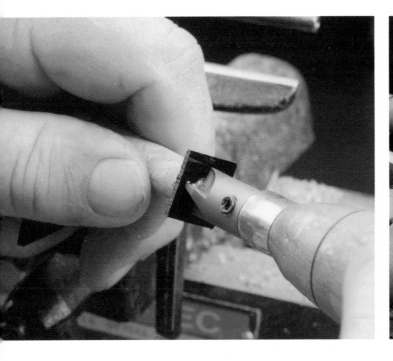 

Use the pen mill to make sure that the brass tube is not protruding beyond the pickguard material. It is also a good idea to chamfer the inside.

Since there are no voids in the pickguard material, it comes off in steady shavings that wrap around the barrels.

You will need to stop and remove the shavings.

Sand and finish as for other pens.

Reduce the blanks to the bushing diameters on the ends

Use the assembly for a standard straight pen.

and to a diameter which is pleasing to the eye in the center.

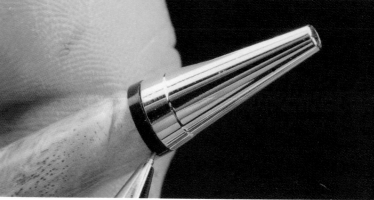

The uniform width of this pickguard accent shows the reason that we went through the exercise of cutting the shoulders and mounting the pickguard after the tubes were glued rather than before.

One Piece Pen and Pencil Set

Again, we would like to create something different—something that will make our fellow craftsman ask, "How did he do that?" In my opinion, this is not the most durable of pens. At the tip end it becomes very thin and prone to cracking since the barrel is not glued to the pen body. The pencil poses no problems as the tubes are glued inside. To strengthen the pen body at the tip, I have glued onto the blank a short section of cast polyester. The glue joint may break since there is not much surface on which to glue, but it is still a fun project.

Scuff up the surface of three tubes for good glue adhesion.

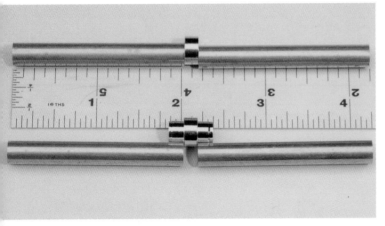

To establish the length of our pencil barrel, we lay both tubes in position with the center coupler.

Glue the polyester disk to the ends of the blanks and drill through.

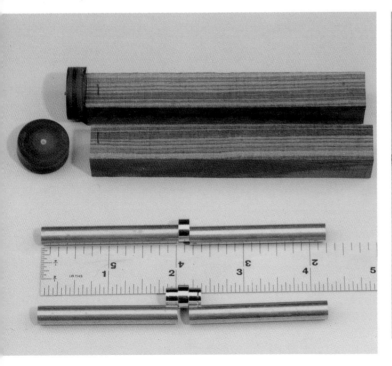

Cut the blanks to the overall length, plus enough to trim at the tubes. I am using Kingwood with black polyester accent. On the top is the pen with the center band between the tubes, which will be the total length of the barrel. Do this with the kit you will be using, as the brass tubes may vary in length.

Determine which blank is for the pen by selecting the truest hole at the tip end by feeling with a brass tube. This blank will not have a tube glued in the tip end. Apply medium density glue to the scuffed tube, rotate the tube in the top or clip end and work it back and forth before setting the depth to ensure the best adhesion possible. Do the same for the other two scuffed tubes in the pencil blank.

Use a pen mill to trim the three ends with tubes glued into them. For the tip end of the pen, insert the loose brass tube to act as a bushing for the pen mill and clean up the end of the pen in the same you have the pencil.

I make a flowing shape so that additional wood can be left to help strengthen the center of the pen where the barrels are not joined. Taper down to the diameter of the bushings at each end. This is especially needed in the pencil as there is a gap between the tubes where the coupler would normally be.

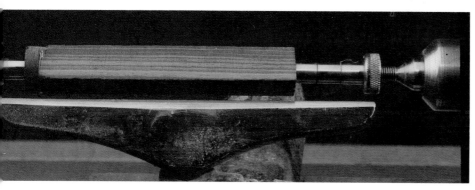
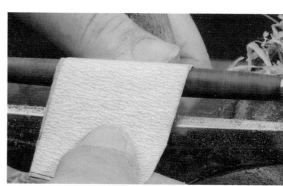

Mount the pen blank on the mandrel. Be sure to put the loose brass tube on the mandrel before putting the blank over it. This will hold it concentric to the axis of the lathe.

Sand and finish.

Reduce the blank.

Mount the pencil blank and follow the same procedure.

When the pencil barrel is finished, check to make sure that it matches the pen.

To assemble the pen align the clip and press home the clip and clip bushing.

The pencil assembly is straight forward. Insert and seat the tip bushing. Put on the clip and clip bushing and seat.

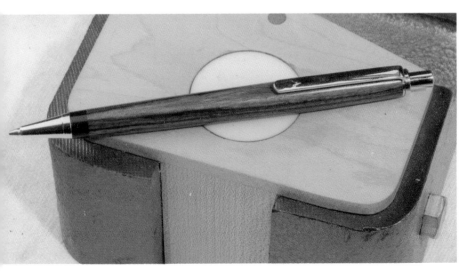

Drop in the transmission and screw on the tip.

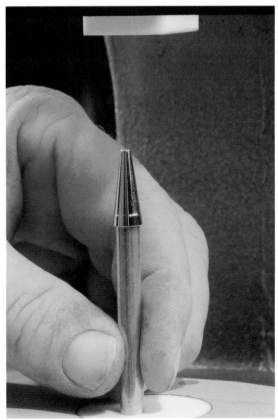

Press the tip into the remaining tube.

Insert the transmission into the other end of the brass tube, and with the help of the height block, seat it to its proper length.

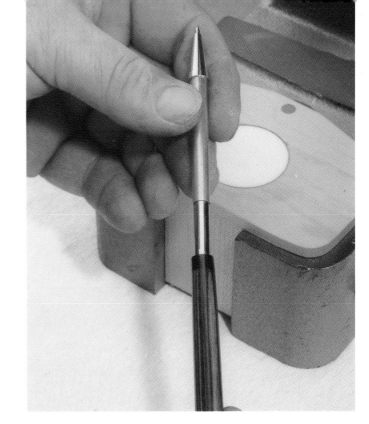

Insert the whole assembly into the bottom of the pen.

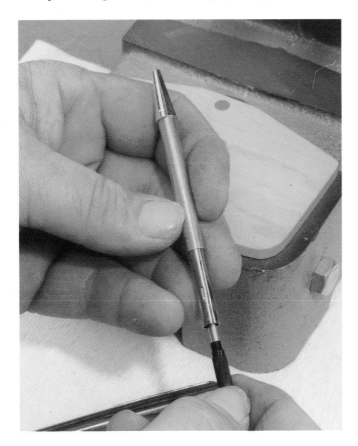

Insert the refill into the transmission.

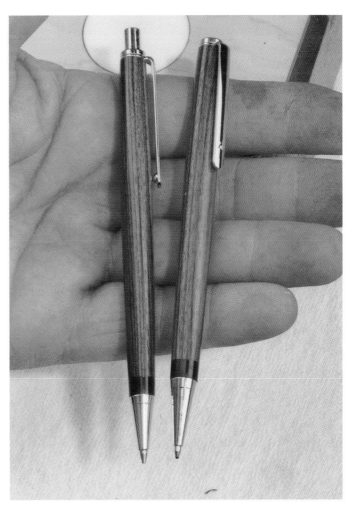

Finished pen and pencil set.

Lanyard Pen

Occasionally people like a pen that's harder to lose. Now we have a pen they can hang around their neck. It is made by using the pen kit for a standard straight twist pen and replacing the clip and clip cap with the fob from a key chain kit. A lanyard or chain can then be run through the fob.

Another option is to make a detachable lanyard pen. For this you need a detachable key chain kit along with the standard straight twist pen kit. The diameter of the pen must be adjusted to match the attachment. Adjustments may be necessary any time we start combining kits.

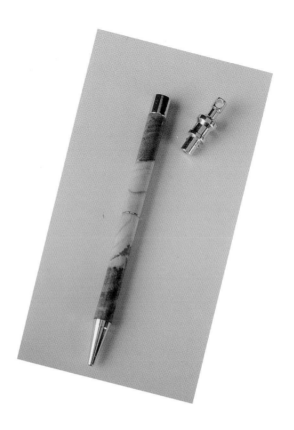

The top comes off so the pen can be used and then reattached to the chain or lanyard.

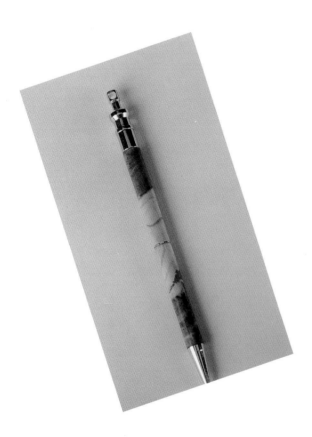

A pen made from spalted cherry with a detachable lanyard attachment. This pen is made using the standard straight twist pen kit and a detachable key chain kit.

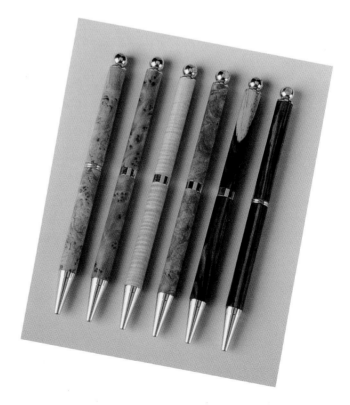

Left to right: Cherry Burl, Thuya Burl, Fiddleback Maple, Amboyna burl, cocobolo with sapwood, cocobolo. These pens are all have key ring tops for lanyards.

Gallery

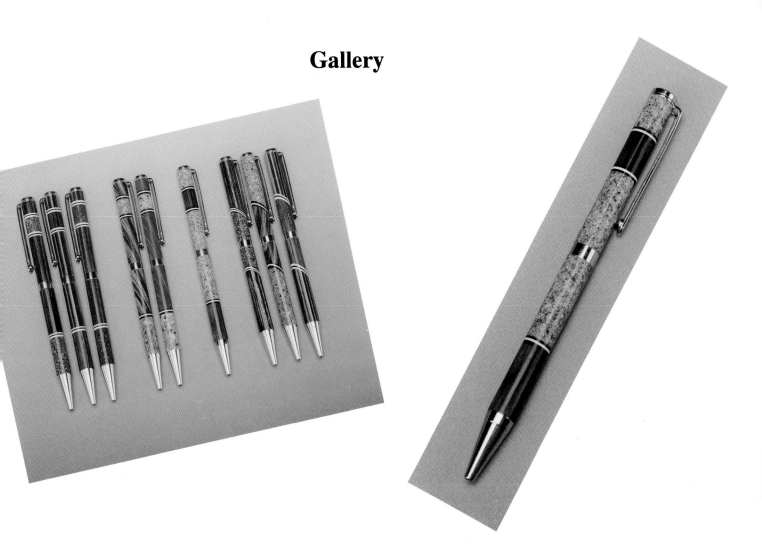

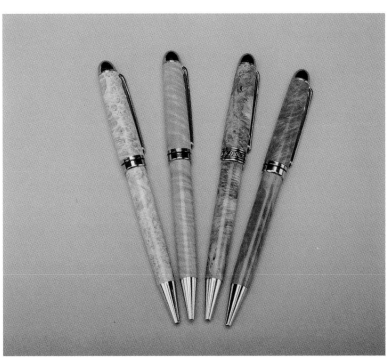

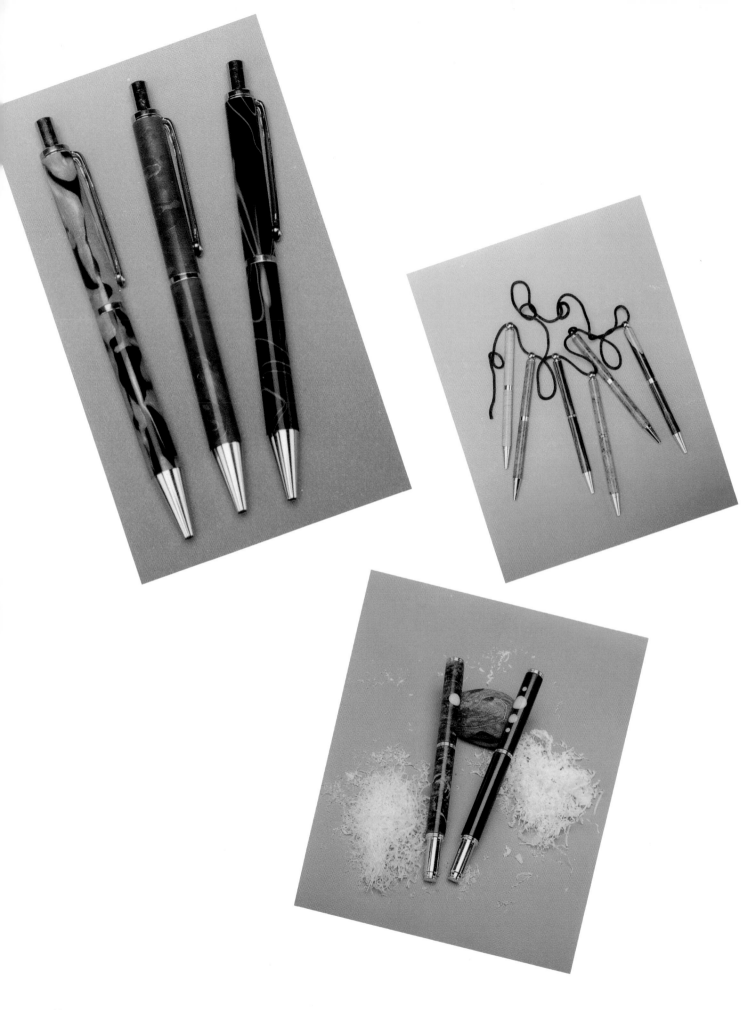

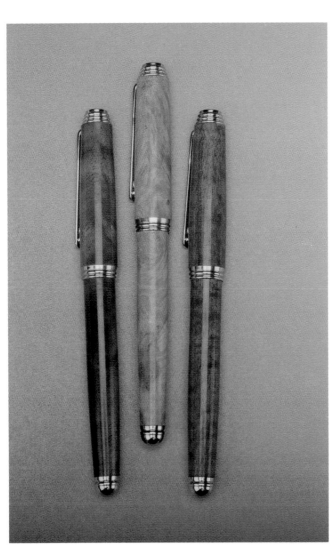

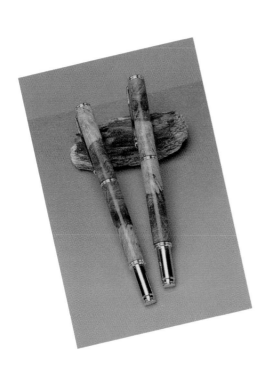

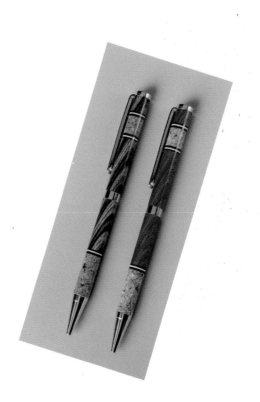

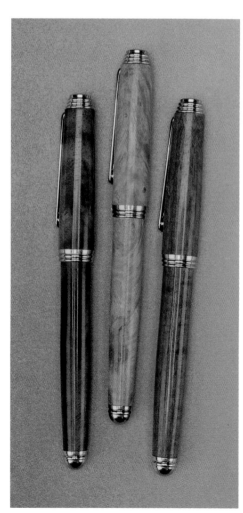

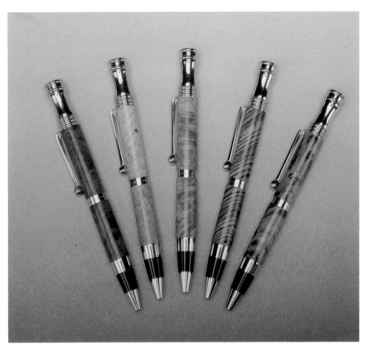